Prayers With a Side of Cash

Prayers With a Side of Cash

by Kathleen Florence

MOON
TIDE PRESS

~ 2025 ~

Prayers With a Side of Cash
© Copyright 2025 Kathleen Florence

Editor-in-chief
Eric Morago

Operations Associate
Shelly Holder

Associate Editors
Mackensi E. Green
Ellen Webre
Allysa Murray

Editor Emeritus
Michael Miller

Front cover art
Kathleen Florence

Book design
Michael Wada

Moon Tide logo design
Abraham Gomez

Prayers With a Side of Cash
is published by Moon Tide Press

Moon Tide Press
6709 Washington Ave. #9297
Whittier, CA 90608
www.moontidepress.com

FIRST EDITION

Printed in the United States of America

ISBN # 978-1-957799-35-3

Contents

III. Magic Hour

I.
Wide Shot

Leaving New York

Big Apple smells sweetest in spring,
on mornings when blossoms bless

Bleecker, hours before that high noon
sun barrels down between

buildings, hitting piss floating
on oil spills. Making shine

spotty sidewalks holding hands
with tired walls. A view best seen

from rooftops, through windows
with fire escapes,

next to an overflowing bookshelf,
Joni Mitchell on a wall.

Reminding you there's an exit sign,
if you pan left, a highway.

A way to leave here gracefully,
before summer strikes a match.

There Are Other Routes Than 66

Because Jack coulda been Jackie,
if tables had been laid differently,
with stories dished to suit
pinker tongues—this songbook of recipes
rides shotgun. Penned by grandmothers
who rode stormy ocean waves,
into beginnings unknown, as if they knew
this life is for going places,
should you want to make it home.

I'm steering my ship with sound.
I've Been Everywhere is loud
for ancestors riding
with me through veins pumping
red—bound to turn purple, burst
into flowers, push through unseen spaces
along paved roads. Smile
through cracked-tooth ditches,
even as they are called *mere weeds.*

As my song list flips from Cash
to Breeders to Alabama Shakes,
I remember names, taught
to me by those with hands in the ground.
Names like Cornflower, Balm Bee,
and my favorite: Dame Rocket.
Yeah, Jack, that's me.

Springtime in the Gettysburg Museum Parking Lot

I went to the Gettysburg Museum yesterday but didn't get far.
Security looked inside my four-inch purse before letting me into
the washroom. Inside, against dark gray walls, sinks and stalls,
teenagers jumping for the camera. Legs kicking, knees bent,
big smiles celebrating life in this prison decor-inspired space
as happily as if on spring break in Aruba. Outside, children
pouring out of yellow buses like gasoline, teachers tsk-tsking,
typical teenager replies, tossing water bottles for footballs under
a great blue sky. White clouds fluffy as dreams over green grass
rolling hills. Magnolias and cherry blossoms getting ready for
the great bird-meets-bee sex adventure. In the parking lot, an old
man holds onto his daughter's arm, as they make their way to
somewhere I'll have to see another time. Can't stick around. The
road calls me with a promise of freedom. In a wide country that
spilled blood so I can spill words, children can spill water, and
girls can jump into cameras capturing freedom anywhere they
please.

Madison Thumbs a Ride

I fall for the wide-legged pants,
two finger peace sign. She is alone
on the road, marketing her resistance
to fear. She is a woman, not a bear,
which we joke about, while wildfires burn
north of Washington, DC.
On her way to see family,
after a decade in San Francisco,
Madison tells me she was ready to be free
after her mother died,
but an older sister rattled in her dream.

She leans out the window when talking
about Summerville. I see that wide,
airy porch, lazy as a Tuesday
afternoon pool table, corner pocket
rocking chair, thirty-minute drive
to ocean. My passenger smiles, saying
this world spins counterclockwise,
so why does our perception of time
move inexorably forward?

This is something to hum about
as traffic turns to midnight,
stranger turns to story,
and lights in the opposite direction
dare to blind me.

The Thing About Alice

other than her name, is the way she stays out of it at the table.
Flying potatoes, green beans, apple pie, and hot sauce

for Uncle Michael, who might be a liberal
in some circles, but not here.

Alice is the only name that doesn't come from the big book,
where cousins Rachel, John, Peter got theirs.

It couldn't be why she isn't like us,
thinks her mother, before pushing back her chair.

Gravy pouring quietly,
fingers fidgeting under the maple,

incapable of saying the things she does
when she is with her friends.

How they could never see, how unfair it is to be
outside, unwanted, dismissed. As if Rachel, John, Peter were

not—hold that thought—table swinging, old man up
to bat. He's gonna say something to send it through the window.

Rushing blood, love this game made simple, two teams
and only one can win. *History is war, pass the gin.*

Alice looks down, carpet patterns peace her eyes,
in lines, color weaving, her teeth tight with being right.

Mother returns with bird baked in its own juice.
Everyone eats but Alice.

Someone refrains from asking *what is wrong with you*?
This is so delicious.

Red Flag

In her twenties she was just like them,
for a while.

Until they formed a circle, hands cupped
in whisper.

Turned their backs to raise a red flag,
warring from deep inside.

To distance those who can't find
their way to fit in.

No matter how they try, in a country
of color, all its own.

Something Borrowed, Something Blue

Let me share a secret, my dear girl, who is not mine
but shares the same color of sky in her eyes.

Your dreams are dancing metaphors,
sacred prayers that can't be shamed away.

They will repeat, replay, rerun, until waking life,
traveling around our sun, ripens in response.

I know those girls in white dresses have been pulling
focus for ages, but a bridal veil is threshold,

not destination. Your garden needs attention.
There are blossoms waiting to apple.

I've seen your dreams—you wear them on t-shirts.
They arrive in lines gathering at the edges of your eyes.

I know this gift isn't on your registry, and belonging
to each other by blood can be messy. Our two dozen years

of history comes down to sharing one hospital chair,
when the doctor opened my dead mothers' eyes.

What else could I give you, than to be with you
when we witnessed the absence of blue?

It is the same gift given to me. You can see it
in our mirrors, shining.

Girls With Heads on Fire

I know girls with heads on fire, who roll out of bed
letting gravity decide if head or feet will find

ground first. Girls who throw punches, crush
fingers with boot, offer rescue to those passing

sideways through hallways, avoiding obvious brutes.
Pushing bullies who won't get out of the way. Girls

who grow into grandmothers, having survived
those trying to blame her for what's between her legs.

Girls who open doors, to life bulging in her belly,
in her hand, in her heart. She paints skies with riddles,

curls hair to be sisters, carries knives to be comrade.
Blessing mornings with softness, kicking excuses

onto the front lawn. She will let you win
with a few extra points. Arranging her hair with flowers,

making friends with a monkey on her shoulder, painting
orchids and skulls in the red earth west. There are girls

who have never been told to be quiet, have never been
shamed into staying silent, and they are very young.

Stillness

Curtains fall,
curtains are rain,
rain is mountain,
mountain is road.
Waiting is red fox,
ready to lead you,
to everyone dancing,
without rehearsal
on stage.
Stage play is dreaming,
incoherent movie,
with actors you knew
a long time ago.
Before credits roll,
before school bell rings,
before day begins.

Motion Picture

I pick up a passenger who takes the wheel as I make a motion
picture with my phone. *Like Soderbergh*, I joke, sort of. Asking
him where he's going. Figure I'll have footage if he pulls a gun.
He spills his story, as if his story could fit into an hour—or was it
two?—driving west. Saying he needs to be free from a house where
he could not sleep. For a moment I wonder if he's really here. But
then, who is driving this car? Camera rolls. Digital wheels spin.
He wants me to believe him. Wants me to give him my attention
as he cuts his own throat, blood seeping into my driver's seat.
Unspoken memories and dreams trapped behind his teeth. His
arms flexed at the wheel. Yellow bullet lines graze his gaze. His
clenched jaw says he's been thinking for days in dark rooms with
pictures he can't unsee. I turn window-side to record scenery. In a
dolly-smooth shot, I capture light and motion in one minute. No
cuts. Big picture. Scene.

The Clearing

In my crazed
and delayed
way of letting
grief
push me
to my knees,
I believed
it was
my mother's spirit
throwing lightning,
splitting
my backyard tree,
which later
was cut down
so I could see
past it.

Before Postmodernism

There is this story. About a woman pressing an iron over clothes. She wrote poetry and won contests that gave her money. In a kitchen of rhymes. This is a time of hand-washed diapers, women marching for equal rights, not unlike today. Heads of departments discussing postmodernism. Death of everything. Cups filled by people without names. Names of men we paid to memorize, write about, reference. Go into debt for. Desperate for inclusion, we learned to scoff at story. Like the one about a woman who wrote poetry, won contests, was paid money, while she gave children three meals a day. Ironing out wrinkles like an editor.

Paper Map

Holding a paper map, someone asks if I'm lost.
Just looking, I say, mishearing their question.

We laugh as a friendship begins. That's how it is
sometimes. Of course, we're not the kind of friends

who will drift apart over time, sending holiday cards
that will sit, get moved to a drawer, box, attic, bin.

It's more like friends I made when I was ten
while on vacation with my parents.

In a place safe enough to be found while hiding,
trading bracelets, telling secrets, feeling new

in someone else's eyes. We didn't need to keep in touch,
we'd never forget each other. At least, that's how it was

with me, taking the map, even though I don't need one.
It's something to hold onto.

Debaser

Talk about settling down,
growing up, getting real,

as if what we are isn't real
but something temporary.

As if that isn't actually
the road we are on,

marked with detours,
U-turns, lanes ending.

We keep believing
there is reason, meaning—

making sense on this highway,
our future singing a chorus.

Blurring verses with bridges,
crossed in places we played,

mistakes we made
were sounds repeated.

Listening like a lake
we came to buoy on,

now a circle on a calendar,
appointments at an office,

fading out instead of ending
the way we ended with a bang.

That Night in Bushwick

Baseball caps, fedoras, knitted shrugs
covering heads, in purple light we are

nodding to beats, string of lights overhead
glow, music on a scenic rooftop.

To get here: an open window one floor below,
scaling a wall to a view

where skyline promises a seat with dreamers
who left somewhere else, just like you.

Someone is making a movie, another in a band,
wringing the old self out into a novel

idea that comes clean in morning,
under covers of lost religion.

A song we all know words to
has a way of catching youth

for a moment, for three minutes,
in a place where we make it forever.

II.
Long Shot

Meditation Highway

No songs, no talking,
        no podcast, for now.
Just this stretch of cool gray,
        miles of cruise control,
periphery of cornfield,
        straw man hanging,
        silver tree jazz-handing,
helped by atmospheric pressure
        off camera.
I count my breaths
        between gas stations,
passing on picking up hikers—
        like that ferry boat driver
        followed by flying monkeys,
        lion with fists of fear
who have fooled me before,
        chattering my ride,
        when all I want is silence
to soundtrack all this cinema.

I Left My Snowbrush in Georgia

Under a full moon swinging on strings
of light, I put my snowbrush down.

No frost to clear come morning,
only sweetgum shedding scars

will fall on my car. This road south
has drowned winter into spring.

An umbrella in my trunk,
an end to white noise.

No more snow days, snowjobs
or Snow White eating apples.

Whites of my eyes are clear, waking
to a stretch of road saying *hello*.

You Are

my first thought waking,

key to new thoughts unlocking,

song that heliums my heart,

slow dance to heaven's stairway,

whole sky getting my attention,

pep in my step, on our walk home.

What Is Writing

but trying to make sense of,
be witness to this holy experiment.
From bug smack on windshield
to your parent's death, there is
feeling, wanting, desire to capture,
reenter this world screaming,
into emptiness that becomes familiar.
Faces coo cooing over you,
what you see,
what you need to put in words.
While people talk of angels—what else
are strangers you come to know?
Or even if you don't,
miraculously,
someone holding you,
holding these words you write,
cares you are alive.

Following Death into Florida

Five

miles

under

this

speed

limit

adds

up

over

time,

but what's time to a dead body?

Flesh rots
while the living write songs on the interstate.

One following another in circles.
I've got my man in black t-shirt on.
I'm following death into Florida.

It turns left,
                         I turn right.

Highway 10 Headstone

Tallahassee bound
      over the historic Swanee River,
      Bugs sang about Saturday morning.
Song raising memory from my mind's cemetery,
      blue-eyed child
      eating cereal on the floor
      in front of the idiot box.
Wheels spin.
      Andy Warhol is there,
      in a big yellow chair.
My banana ripens on this dashboard.

Ava of America

She is a cool girl in knee-high red boots, fringe hanging from the rim of her sequined hat. It's an act and she's on break, fake-smoking Marlboros out back, where I've wandered looking for my car. She asks where I'm heading. I tell her. Wait for the line about catching a ride, but it doesn't come. She doesn't ask where I'm from. Instead, she wants to know if I'm on the run. If I'm *an outlaw*. I hook a thumb in the small pocket of my decade-old skinny jeans and answer *no*. She holds my gaze. Looking to see if I really am a rebel without a cause. I lift my chin to say I'm full of causes. Brimming with reasons. It's only been sixty years since passing the equal pay act—women are still paid less than men. She inhales her cigarette. It comes back out slowly. Her mouth a smoking gun. Never breaking eye contact in a showdown between girl on stage and girl watching. We are the same person at this moment.

Tornado Country

My wipers keep a steady beat,
my tune hums underneath

the beat of this small city square.
I see flag-wavers,

out in rain with megaphones,
hats that say:

I wish things were like the old days,
when women knew their place.

Ladies in a car next to me stare
too, wondering what century

this state is in, where
the next off ramp is,

as if leaving will here
will solve the problem.

Billboards from Alabama to Louisiana

You feel water rising, up to your praying knees.
You see promises of salvation, but not Banksy.

You see highway signs from Whiskey Bay
to Bayou Bridge. Mixed in with shouts

for *fast food, casino, payday loans*—is Jesus.
Pictured with shoulder-length hair, look

of love for everyone who dares
see him. One sign salutes a lawyer's promise

to protect the rights of the injured.
Vote for me, it says. Vote for me.

Long Haul

Some states take a full day to cross.
Stopping for gas in hamlets built

on dreams of being destinations.
Some have summer-place status.

They are potato-salad kind of towns,
waving family nostalgia flags.

Filled with pretty houses batting
their eyes under empty blue skies.

It's 2024. This country's door is still open,
but there's more than a whiff of what's

to come, of what's already come undone.
We are moving through an age

of misinformation, national frustration,
fear of the unknown. Tapping into

artificial intelligence for artificial times.
People talk.

Who's going to change this two-party
system? Is there another option?

Country built on stories bulldozed
by billboards of *us* versus *them.*

Who's going to fight us? ask
dangling effigies. Bullies spell

it out: *you will be dead if you have*
no clout. No money. No connections.

The wrong color skin.
If you say the wrong thing.

Will people without power
be okay if they stray

too far from man holding
leash, walking dogma?

This earth is heating to boil—stolen soil
keeps getting bought in recession.

Tension rising in streets, parking lots,
over property, plots, little towns just like this.

What about me?
What about us?

I look around, checking my sideview,
rearview mirrors. Look for unity signs.

Hands on this wheel keep me from spinning.
Reflection on the bright road ahead hits me.

There's still so much missing,
still so much future to go.

My Friend Is Collecting Wheels

First motorbike, then summer camper.
Before that, truck as big as three bumper cars,
smashed around at the fair. She buys
and sells wheels like a hobby. Cruises
along rivers, top down, shifting
gears in mountains—trading
it all in for a minivan, sleeping
on the beach come summer.
She doesn't hashtag vanlife.
There are no sponsors for products.
Jenny is a one-woman band with a cellphone,
calloused fingertips from nights spent learning
guitar, again. She's an old friend,
who always answers when I call.

Thick Skin Bias

She is not walking into an ocean, acclimatizing to a hot
summer day. Her skin will not grow armor, poor people

do not have thicker skin. Poverty does not make us
stronger, there is no badge of honor given at the shelter.

We will not get used to it. We do not need less help,
less love, or less attention, because our homes are smaller,

shoes are older, or a car is marked by accident
we cannot afford to fix.

Prayers with a side of cash will not be answered faster
to suit the comforts of others.

Those prayers are not better, or more important
than anyone who owns less junk.

This culture schooled in nostalgia for waste,
fake love and plastic compassion have thick skin bias,

middle-class credit card debt, neurotic nursery rhymes
keeping us all up late at night. Sugar plum stories

about pulling up bootstraps, benefits of hard knocks,
and this dream realized, if we work a little harder.

Never mentioning those who must lose,
for those who will win. From cemetery rows

to unpaid alimony, sacrifice sounds nice
on a Sunday with a choir.

Cinema Paradiso

In a small town that I will probably never see again, I stop at a food truck, in the parking lot of a big-name hardware store. Picnic tables sprinkled over a slice of grass. An eighty-year-old man asks me to join him. I bring my take-out over. Battered fish and deep-fried chips. Extra sides of slaw and pickles. I settle in and listen to his story for more than an hour.

It feels like talking to my dad, again, in a way. On those days when we were happy to see each other and careful not to say things to upset that hive of bees.

He's retired. His wife died. His children moved away. Where else would he go, he wants to know. He has his steady routine. I nod and smile and talk about the miles I've put between me and my past. He doesn't ask overly personal questions. We finish our fries, now chilled, as sky darkens. Other tables empty.

It's said you can't really know a place just passing through, but I see the same movie has been playing at the cinema for eight weeks straight. At a run-down building I stop to photograph. Wish good luck. Walking back to my car, I notice a patch of weeds the town has yet to mow down. A garden of bee food offering so much more than manicured lawns. That's how it is here. There's only so much room for wilderness.

What's Playing at the Apocalypse Theatre

It's Tuesday and zombies are moving through streets

again,
across movie screens hunting Iggy Pop.

                  I drift and think about

r e v o l u t i o n
talked about in hole-in-the-wall cafes.

Taxpayers at work, man evicted from his apartment now listed
as an air be or not to be. In some near future,

downtown streets lined with tents, people paying rent
to make movies, in a city the world loves to stalk. Talk

show that loves to talk about a world that is e n d i n g.
It's always ending, and the dead don't die. They keep eating minds

while we sit in this cave eating popcorn and our world outside
e x p l o d e s.

If War + Peace Was a Hit on Netflix

If Napoleon was Donald Duck,
if Donald Duck was Daffy,
if Duckie wasn't John Cryer,
if we only knew who the liar in the room was,
would it change things?
If John Snow was Snow White,
if Snow White played White Stripes,
at a party where 7 dwarves,
are 7 horsemen of the apocalypse—
name of that actor is on your lips.
If we weren't so caught up with numbers,
with figures, we'd trip out on the brain,
mapping tunnel secret funnel to a rainbow.
If a rainbow was a poem to rain,
a clothesline for bigots to dry out their pain.
If pain was paint to put on the wall,
if the wall had fallen before it was erected,
if an erection was affection and never a weapon,
if weapons came forward to make amends,
if endings stopped pretending to end,
if peace was the meaning of friend.
If *War and Peace* was a hit on Netflix,
if Netflix and chill had been code for plague,
if Margaret Thatcher was Billy Bragg,
if Billy Bob Thorton had stayed in the band,
Like a boomerang, I need a repeat.

Texas Is an Extra Large Pizza

Texas is an extra-large pizza painted red.
There are no pineapple pieces here,

but specialty coffee and hop-infused water
are sides dressed in blue,

sneaking up on tractors and trucks.
Passing on this long-haul drive,

is sheriff side eye, yellow highway lines,
lassoed to one white puffy cloud ahead.

This state is a boat without water,
sky without shade,

tiny white clapboard church flag
as big as a three-story hotel.

Texas is *The Last Picture Show*
colorized and selling pottery.

Antiques, boutiques, soy candles,
whiskey-infused sweetener.

Every small town is a showdown
between settlers and California creep.

It's everywhere. Artists changing
neighborhoods, artsy raising

rural into destinations,
where hillsides are painted white.

Pilgrim-bleached bones
under hellfire sun that says SMILE.

Texas is an unclimb-able tree,
dried out rocky root off-limits sign,

it's a picnic stop without table,
an hour between gas stations,

water sprinkler bylaw,
state with one natural lake,

tough-horned bull on thirsty ranch,
dotted yellow, purple flowers come spring.

It's a flat balloon cacti, spiked with David Lynch
repeating *congratulations, safe travels, all the best.*

Texas is a bug flying into my windshield,
telephone pole shaped like a cross,

cloud watching from passenger's side,
shapes flying under big top moving at great speeds.

Though from down here, it's as if they are pillows,
for un-yet imagined thoughts,

getting ready to burst
into raising our flowers.

Texas is a five o' clock shadow,
moving across land of a pimply-faced boy,

a lonely ranch boy fixing his one red wagon,
to pull that lode star into another night.

Texas is a spectrum of green to sand, going east
to west, all the way to last chance El Paso.

Praying for Peace

World on fire and people are sending
thoughts and prayers.

What else to do, but wave
around a stadium together

at half-time? Raise consciousness
like a roof or a fundraiser.

Who prays for our sisters' lives?
Who prays for bullies to put down

knives? Guns? Fists? Who prays
for resistance?

How much does a question cost
without an answer to pay?

Answers said like a toast,
like grace, like a blessing.

Glenda Travels Light

It's her seashell bracelets that catch my attention. Her tiny
backpack, smell of patchouli oil, that isn't strong. She isn't going
too far, and I am tired. My thoughts are starting to feel like
a phonograph. So I invite Glenda to come along and she tells
me about making her way around the world one country at a
time. Fresh from Africa, she shows me drawings on her phone,
as everything she owns has been given away or is at her mother's
home in Santa Barbara. She is sixty, unmarried, unlike women
who throw showers for babies. She's off to Tibet next, but first,
a stop to see an old friend who lives in the desert and tells fortunes
over the internet. I share my lunch with Glenda. She tells me
about bartering in Fiji. It all feels so simple, so light. And yes,
sometimes she is lonely, peeling the banana slowly, she adds *that's
grief.* It comes and goes. A good talk helps to lighten the load.
The silence that follows in my car smells of summer pavement
after rain.

One Day You Will Be Old

One day you will be old and need help bathing, while your
unusable mouth calls for water.

One day you may have to listen to others too terrified by silence,
or the waiting it takes for you to answer.

One day your car may stall, your license stolen, your everyday
decisions swiped clean by the mop of life's cruel janitor.

Downward this hill that has no gratitude, for all the lawns you
cut, or nights you stayed up waiting for that child to finally come
home.

One day and then, will the promise of the next world fill your
lungs, while others collect their memories in shopping malls?

You can't always be thinking of the future, but one day isn't that
all you will have?

In a Hospice Parking Lot

Knowing someone will die today punctuates my morning,
stronger than coffee brewing in the kitchen, where the cook is
making food for mouths that might not eat.

A fork lets out steam in a pent-up pie, and I step inside where beds
on wheels are steered by nurses and later funeral staff.

When it's time, workers form a line on both sides of the hall, like
dandelions pushing up color through a narrow crack between
sidewalk and grass

for the family who follows body covered in cloth, gently rolled to
parking lot, where a woman, my age, meets my eyes and thanks
me in a glance for this

simple act of being here—we bouquet around the family as the
body slides into the back of a minivan, someone we never knew
but are here for.

What We Need

Light switch needs light bulb,
baby toe needs heel,
child needs their parent,
without clouds, sun would burn earth.
Hair needs ear to tuck itself behind,
so face that needs smile can be seen.
Bells need listening,
night needs darkness,
sleep is impossible during a rave.
When we say we need each other,
we are talking about water
we are all part of,
clouds and lakes,
little feet we call rain.

This Poem Is

a love note written on paper covered in woodsmoke
scent, where it stayed in a bag you carried

over your shoulder. This poem is waiting to be felt
in your mouth, soft, with tongue, to make sounds

a poem makes, when it has been given time to form.
This poem is four lines painted on a road, five lines

holding notes, ten lines if you count the treble,
thirty lines to mark a month. This poem is a sign

for romance, private party invitation, ceremony
so sacred, only a witness of one can read it

at a time. This poem is writing with one hand, while
the other reaches in darkness, unsure if separation creates

balance or longing for what's missing. Bending
into a recognizable shape, an image in late afternoon,

this poem is two lights facing each other, shining
up space in between.

Diners and Dive Bars

Charlie sits next to me in the booth
while a waitress in blue
pours coffee like a movie.

> Orange rim on plastic pot,
> green seats in frame.

He's tucked into my bag,
brown button eyes looking up at me.

> I made him at camp with help
> from a lady sewing his card

board mouth. It still opens when I
put my hand up his shirt, my fingers
touching the soft stuff inside.

> Dive bar in Austin, an audience of three
> waiting for him to say something funny.

He's a puppet, I explain.
The waitress gets it. She sees
this sort of thing all the time.

11 Places I've Waited

Next to a phone from the last century,
against a wall of hopeful flowers
      where my mother danced,
at a terminal of missed connections,
in a parking lot watching my brother
      drive away,
beside my father as he lay dying,
inside a classroom hard with rules,
lingering next to a coffin,
      but not for too long,
below a horizon of dark
      moments before light blooms,
at a point in the story I've marked
with an envelope,
before I open this letter unread,
after I press send.

Monologue

Waiting at the crossroads wondering if you ran out of fuel,
got a flat, left the road, got distracted.

If I go looking, I might get lost too.
I've been lost before and it can take forever to find the road

again. Maybe you've found a dancehall—
pretty flowers pressed against the wall.

Pink Gerber, Brown-eyed Susan, a lily for your sorrow,
waiting for your beautiful eyes to see them.

Maybe you like the soft offering of a flower's cheek,
your feet inside spaces of each other's feet,

heat of another body
when you haven't felt heat all this time.

Almost anyone would understand why you wandered,
broke curfew for a chance to dance.

And what will you say,
when you walk away?

Flower in that pink dress is probably already in love with you
before the band has put guitars in their coffin-shaped cases.

I am pulling on your shirt sleeve, waiting
for you, darling. And you're late.

III.
Magic Hour

At the Intersection of Wonder and Dust

There's a house in Las Cruces with a sunset in the window and a
dog that barks eternally at an emerald couch. Gas station within
walking distance is playing disco. Leonard Cohen is smoking
a cigar. From this kitchen window we see him, across the yard
covered in dust. Later, we sit in chairs wondering what inspired
the pictures on these walls. Remember stories of an unnamed
woman no one wanted to pull from the tavern of darkness for fear
of getting lost inside. We will think of a ringmaker in Santa Fe,
and a second aunt in Taos. At the other end of this line, we will
find them, blessing doorways with welcome mats. Offering gold
rings to replace promises for what no longer exists.

Planted

You plant a kiss behind my ear
as if it were the last seed in earth's darkest magic.

I carry it with me, thinking of a picture your father kept.
You, at seventeen, laughing.

I wonder what that place was you held in your smile,
without a trace of cruelty.

Somewhere in between then and now came worry.
Doubting joy, trading it in for a microwave.

It isn't only stuff, or being free of things.
It's to be free from the fear of missing

out on things we think make us belong.
That's what's missing from your teenage mug.

Laughing, in a band. You did belong
to them, like you belong to us now.

In every dream, in every family, it returns.
A place to plant our magic.

A drop in the earth, an ear that is bending,
to keep our world round, to keep us together.

Leaving Them to Grow

We are gardeners
moving earth in each other.
Making a place for life to rise
in rooms open to sky.
We leave these flowers to grow,
let them sweeten walks.
They don't belong to us,
just this shared heart glowing.
Four rooms connected:
breath to blood to pulse.

Greta's GOAT Farm Cottage

Roads lead back, back, back to goat farm cottage. Rusted trucks,
trailers lining this perpetual summer beat as we make our way to
a gated driveway. An anxious hippie looking like Greta Gerwig
greets us at feeding time. Goats are bleating. Dirt dark as coal in
her fingernails, she talks about her PhD—buying this property
to avoid paying city rent. Mortgage with four goats and now she
feeds three dozen. Farm run by volunteers, cats, a slow-moving
bulldog. There is no crossroad, no corner store to walk to, no field
of pretty flowers, no tourist draw. Just goats, guzzling their heads
at us for affection.

Sliding a Sonic into a Sonnet

You are the first to hit a sweet home run.
Sliding together into that fourth base,
the place nobody calls fourth base because
home base is where we start and where we end.

    Even first base is a murky definition.
    Who is strictly kissing, eyes closed, lips wishing
    in this first stanza for no strike out call?
    Does kissing start here, or where we start swinging at the ball?

Second base has touching and what might be
bumping around in clothes, no one knows if
any of it is below the belt—with
the pitcher's back to you there's some room for

    improvisation.

Third base is simply the great mystery,
it's where Abbott and Costello will find me,
watching from the bleachers my favorite
confusion, *I don't know*, the most common

    frustration.

    If you ask Why they're left outfield,
    or because is in the center of an explanation,
    tomorrow will throw you off balance,
    for what today is catching.

Logic follows the shape of a diamond—
four times to run, four slides into the base,
three times to strike out, eight ways to call it,
but only one way to hit it out of

    the stadium.

It's what makes people cheer, makes us rise and
sit and rise again in waves, it's the way.

    It's what makes us hug strangers,
    spill beer, slap backs, high five,
    paint ourselves in matching colors
    for the day.
    That's what it means to get to fourth base.
    It's the prize for returning.
    It's all this coming together for love.

Truth or Consequences

We take the 10 and miss
Truth or Consequences.

A cool name, you say, *but*
there's nothing worth stopping for.

And I wonder if we stopped
at Truth or Dare,

which one you'd take.
I say dare,

but you say truth, because
you're comfortable where you are.

I fall back into consequence,
our smallest fingers touching.

Skulls and Flowers

I am road around water,
river beside myself,
bending string in winding song,
breath that pulls your rug away.
You are where I want to sleep,
where I want to stay.
I will keep going, the way trees bend
long after you think there's no more wind.
I will be curve in your fists,
spit in your shouts,
dance in your knees.
I see how they bend to me.
I am the one you ask please.
I am your place
where skulls and flowers grow.

Rancho Mirage

Out here my thoughts are twinged
with twang, clear as bleach-bone Zen.

I haven't seen a traffic jam, schoolyard
or hospital in days. But that's the highway.

Ghost towns winking as we drive by.
Stopping for gas we pass a ranch with signs

promising happiness in grass-fed beef,
organic eggs and all the stars in the sky.

I've seen this kind of place before:
house with revolving doors—open to workers,

not owners. For us, there are still a thousand
miles ahead to what we will call home.

The Road Back

Entrance guarded by black raven,
red dirt road leading to starry sky,

and whatever you bring with you
into the galaxy of what's next.

A billion destinations starting with
your own mind's launch pad,

funded by what's carried
in the heart.

If that sounds too woo-woo,
come see me at the winding road,

that takes you to the untangle place.

Your list is meaningless.
When will you put it down?

Edge of the Universe

White light burning,
fire hydrant helium,
oxygen carbon neon,
iron avocado.

You cannot land here, eclipse.

Every 11 or 22 years
magnetic fields outward-flow,
solar wind.

Dipolar, solar spiral sunspots,
minima found in rings of trees,
rings to please the fingers.

Life span—double or nothing.
Life span of ten billion years.

Is ten billion years enough?

Getting hotter, supernovae.
Shockwave from compression,
collapse under gravity,
rotate, make heat.

Our sun orbits the center of the Milky Way.
A galaxy that doesn't orbit anything.

Anything doesn't know itself.

What's your cosmic address?

Have I seen you here before?

Four main pulls:
Saturn, Uranus, Jupiter, Neptune.
Suffering, desire, detachment, path.
Four faces, four horsemen,
foremothers, foretold.

Four birds and tame them.
Four hills from the father.
Four will summon them home.

Pottery of sun people,
chambers, legs, limbs.
Stages of metamorphosis—
typical movements in a symphony.

The one we are writing,
the one I play for you,
the one you sing in my rib.

Add, subtract, multiply, divide,
leap year spectacle, side by side.
Lunar directions playing cards,
highways, cube, medicine wheel,
spinning on earth's axis,
revolving around our sun,
which orbits an ellipse round.

Center of the Milky Way,
pulled toward Andromeda,
pushed around inside supercluster Laniakea.

Nothing is stationary.
Gas clouds, dust grains,
black holes, dark matter.

Are we turtles?
Are we flush?
Are we speeding up, in between
regions of densities, dates,
corners and whys?

In the ever-expanding black box theater,
four legs, four wheels, four-letter word,
you are my dialogue dream,
exploding with me the greatest show yet.

Dollar Store Death Doula

Signs warn to pass with care,
a dollar store death doula rises
from road heat ahead.

Holding her left elbow,
right knee bent at Little Dry Creek.
Is she in yoga pose?

Her hair dark as night swimming,
clothing reflecting fish water—
I realize all the birds are elsewhere.

Until the next crossing,
when she disappears,
sun landing on my sun.

Spotted hands held in prayer,
I wonder if I've seen her before,
on the label of an agave bottle.

You pull over to pee in a canyon.
I haven't seen a billboard
since Texas.

Grand Canyon

Behind a pink tour bus, we stop at a gift shop
where round seniors step out into sunshine,
headed for another magnet on the fridge.

All of us out here on red roads, learning fringe
ideas, cutting through sage, writing lines
in this land of telephone pole wires.

Triangle connections, unseen satellites, stories
coming through. This great trek north is a sea
of people, cars lined up for miles.

To capture snapshots of each other before clouds
roll in. Pictures to say we were here, photographs
to say we are alive.

Koi Pool in a Local Restaurant

Waiting for our table, watching koi lap
in a black marble lobby pool.

Big swish by big fish, while a loud voice
gets a little louder at the bar.

You and me tossing pennies, not noticing
a sign that says *don't throw coins in the water.*

All day we've been seeing white-haired couples
kissing. FREE signs all over town.

Those hours we laughed with your daughter,
me mistaken for a mother

by an old man walking on titanium knees
in a museum full of paintings.

I used to see them in a textbook
with passages still waiting to be read.

Like a martyr,
and for what?

In the tiny ponds of this world
time is oxygen thin,

and oysters fat with envy
will never open.

It Is a Blessing

May these days pass slowly,
the way cacti grows slowly,
the way sun warms the mountain,
olive trees where once almonds grew.

May our days here be blessed
with kind coo dove song,
cicada buzz and chickens
bringing fresh eggs into the world.

May these cloudless skies,
summer kisses and deep sea moonlight
walking in white flower gardens,
give us peace,
help us sleep,
make us stronger in our Sunday faith.

Where wild rabbit dancing
on graves of ghost singing,
the mystery we've traveled
four thousand miles to fill our dreams.

Along a dried riverbed,
into a city of doorways bending to the sun,
our hands find each other in darkness,
and God is known again.

An old friend,
the goodness that keeps us safe,
it is a blessing.

Camera

Can you be impartial? Used by directors
to prove there's a monster lagoon,

hero and threshold, call to adventure,
suffering in black and white?

Confusing exits as endings
rather than kneecaps bending to meet the earth.

It's not your fault—you are part of the everything
road and elbow, ocean and eyelash.

We spiral into each other, into light
as it moves, but what can you do?

That thing you took stays the same,
only how we see it changes.

Camera, you can be obscure
but never without abetting a making of history.

So human in your artificial capture,
you are a poem, a film, a beautiful flaw, you see?

Artists I Know

live in old buildings, open studios spaces,
have slept in strange places,

on sunken couches, long after a certain age.
They make friends with pigeons, carrying

around work in bags, pulled
into coffee shops, where there is heat.

Artists I know wear tight shoes
for their own opening,

when they are young and full of potential.
Friends at the cheese table grinning,

this is really living the dream.
Artists I know have picked groceries

from dumpsters, swiped paper from posters,
exchanging collages with a pal.

Jealous and ambitious, working morning hours,
waking before the sun.

They preach on city corners, run
madly in midnight hours, tell you stories

that will make your heart burst.
Artists I know drum songs with chopsticks,

improvise in kitchens, on subways, in parks.
Those who have grown old know fool's gold,

making a life that has no hero, unless bird
in tree be hero, making mentor of a rising sun.

Artists I know stop, say hello, text, message,
photograph, ignore. They never go anywhere,

never see anyone, never tell you jack shit
about how they feel, until they are on stage.

Playing a part, instrument, showing up in their own
photograph, scribbled drawing, first film.

Sending postcards to each other, and to their family
for a while, but then that stops because some family

never say thank you for your art. Artists I know have
cried themselves to sleep, lonely, alone, wondering

why some people have all the luck, why some
have good parents and others don't.

Artists with no arms and no legs who have painted
landscapes, boats, waves—others who carry their life

on their backs, moving from one place to another
when rent gets too high again.

Teaching other artists to dance by lifting their arms,
never saying *that is wrong* or *do it this way*,

but rather *do it again and again.
Do you love it? Do what you love.*

I know artists who hate what they do for a while,
for a time, and then fall in love again, in that moment

when falling in love is possible,
when mind finds bridge. I know

artists who burn bridges, slam doors, quit jobs,
get fired, break chairs, marry, carry divorce,

have children and leave their spouse when death comes.
Some that sing on city streets, sing to a half-baked moon,

talk to aliens, break traditions, carry a torch, contradict,
start fights, fall in love once again and join celibacy school

as a sign of protest. Artists who wash cars on street corners,
have day jobs and still believe.

I know artists who sleep under moon's uncertainty,
wake up in storms and start again.

What Stays in Vegas

Highway, blue sky,
mountain range hotel,
motel 40 ouncer,
gas station plaid,
flannel park RV,
reservation jewelry,
double or nothing bet.

It's superstar drive,
under a red hot sun.

This town is a holiday,
it's a drive-through wedding,
it's a woman in a parka,
with a dog in the back
of a covered truck, holding a sign.

Her face says: *I had to leave.*
There's no shelter there—
no tree to sleep under,
shed to stand in,
when demon dust clouds climb
six stories high.

Twist their way
across the land—
who is my shelter?
her sign whispers.
Whatever you can spare.

It doesn't ask. It tells you.
It begs.

Singing in Unison

When all churches
have gardens
with food to feed hunger,
when we can grow
what we eat
without permit or poison,
when we give
without need for receipt,
and no one is without
home or safety,
then we can measure
thickness of walls.
See if they hold up.

Highway With a Side of Angel's Motel

We roll up to record this place, falling
for the Johnny Cash cadillac shining

under the motel sign missing an "a",
it came down during a recent windstorm.

So hip, we agree, collect the room key,
for a room unextraordinary, but holy clean.

You nap and I brush my teeth in the next room
where I hear an acoustic guitar through metal vent,

a neighbor's three-chord waltz and singing—
have I heard this before in a Coen Brothers movie?

It moves me to climb on top of the vanity
press my ear into the voice of someone I hope is in love.

I am a priest in a confessional waiting
for the next murmur of some solo heart's desire

when you wander in wondering what it is
I'm listening for, way up here.

Now we're both balancing in socked feet,
sweetly keeping each other from slipping

when all is quiet—too quiet—as if the singer
is listening back.

Our eyes widen, we stop breathing and hear a whisper:
holy ones behold they come, I hear the voice of wings

you spring back shocked and I swallow a laugh
until we are in the next room, falling

into bed kissing, letting all our words and letters go.
Harmonizing until we angel into one sweet song.

Sun Worship

I wake with my hands
kissed by sun
      your face on my stomach.
I wake and we are
sound of church bells
      falling into water.
Roses heavy with pink
in each other.
      You find me
      in my daydreams,
lay sunshine on my face,
and the red in my hair
      comes out
to meet you.

Lake Somewhere

We are moths opening our wings
in this second shot dream,

carrying pulse in our chests,
on our wrists.

If we can breathe without panic.
If we can know rhythm of peace,

share it like air, then the past
will unhook itself from here

and we will be free
from roads to somewhere.

Returning to ourselves,
effortlessly facing sky.

The One That Still Gets to Me

The year Radiohead released *OK Computer,*
I figured out how to play "Karma Police"
on acoustic guitar—but it was always
"Paranoid Android" that got to me,
orchestra pitches after the second bridge
from a great height in harmony, yeah,
baby, that still gets to me, after three decades.

Last night we were blasting down the highway
when it came on and once again it hit,
but in a different way, singing it with you,
knowing it gets to you too—I can tell
by the way you turn that volume up
at the moment when mass is needed—
you're so into it, so free to really feel it.

When we pull into our parking spot you
do not stop, don't turn the key off,
and that's what makes this work for us,
what makes us kindred souls you say,
we agree what is sacred can't be cut off
before it's complete, that no song
is over until we hear what we need.

Fresh Pain

Behind the supermarket,
reverse graffiti.

Last letter on the sign *fresh paint*
is covered with white.

Making me laugh and wonder
if this small gesture was meant to be funny,

and if it's the words that hurt us,
when words aren't always what we remember.

Sometimes it's something missing
that makes it fresh.

Driving My Father's Car

Today is not last week, I am not driving
my father's car. Behind the hearse, along the river.

It took twenty years to arrive at the plot.
No birds the entire time, not one single bird.

Today, I am not watching
terror wrap its fingers around his heart.

I am not offering comfort to my mother's friends,
gathered in a church hall eating

white bread sandwiches. Today, I am not standing
with a small plate of cauliflower, listening

to a humming room of white-haired people
refilling cups of coffee. Standing, barely, by a cool

brick wall, half-hearing my cousin's husband tell me
about the smell of Russian coffee, his march to war.

His poetry unwritten under the roof of someone
who said that stuff is for homosexuals.

Today I am not putting away clothes
that were tossed over a wooden chair

at the end of a bed. I am not washing a nightgown,
folding it gently, to put away, only to be taken out

later and sent exactly *where?* I want to hear you
tell me again about the birds in the neighbor's tree,

cat in the window watching. How you wish someone
would call. I won't name names.

You can't change a mind. You can't pull a hook
from the fish without leaving a hole.

Mother

At our crumbling river wall,
sun falling, we stand with birch—
slender, white, strong.

Leaning into wind, watching
geese fly south again.
Why was I in such a hurry?

Where else could I have wanted
to be but standing with you,
watching those birds, watching
that sky?

I felt the list of things to do,
dinner to make, he'll be waiting—
let him wait.

We are trees, we are birds,
we are whole books held together
long enough to write words,

paint lines. Fall in love,
if we are lucky.
If there is luck.

Walking Barefoot in L.A.

Walking north on Larchmont
in flowing white clothes,
white of her linen,
white of her feet—
flashes memory.

My dream the night before,
I went looking for my mother
six years after she died.
White sheers on a window
between me and this empty seat.

Flimsy division.
Morning meditation asking me
to locate the furthest sound away.
I heard thunder.
Now, I hear saxophone,
while a woman walks
barefoot on concrete and sun shines
white light on my hands again.

Weighted Words Are

Stones in Virginia's pockets,
letters arriving late in William's red wheelbarrow,
images that keep falling from memory's library shelf.

Rose petals a small girl tosses to the wind,
and there they go skipping down the road again.
Road which is a river we are floating along.

Carried to a dance hall, strawberry-kissed real,
no more yesterday's wish and Joni song
sung in the key of heart on sleeve.

How many more verses does one need
to find a pink sunset sky after the rain,
a dream-painted sleeping, bringing us here?

Old Lady Yoga

I joke,
scanning the floor of people over thirty posing corpse,
wondering if, and what if and what about—
hush now
and be a rock the size of your palm at the bottom of a stream.
Water moving both ways,
all ways around you looking up,
see that light?
Now sink deeper into everything changing.
You are not a rock but for now you can be
feeling the flow of moment passing you by.
If you can sink deeper and let the mouths of the hungry
suck your surface for substance, then maybe you can be a poet.
But if you are found with your head in the oven
don't expect bread to rise, baby doll,
the voice message said.
Like a first line in a new play,
where the narrator adds
every moment is a first kiss
if you let it.

Cause to Eat Oranges

Here they are. Given away freely. Samples at Sunday's market. Large pieces, cut in triangles, bright as carnivals, ready to eat. It takes teeth to tear away what's inside. It takes a strong tongue to crush this sweetness into the roof of my mouth, where summer stings fresh. Oranges picked yesterday. So different from the ones I knew back east that took weeks to reach a supermarket shelf. Slumped by a long ride in dark boxes that faded their flavor every hour. These oranges are ready to release themselves into the world today. Into a mouth that isn't hungry but is asking for joy. Yesterday, I heard a man say he won't write about flowers or birds until rules are shaped to the arc of his foot. I wonder at how the ground keeps rounding as we keep walking and words keep finding ways to ripen. Here they are. Here they are.

Wave Up

Before our bodies give up breath,
final exit—stage right,

our eyes stop seeing fine lines
on the faces of friends.

This is why we look the same
as we did when we were children.

We are blind with love.
What other way is there to be?

As we wave goodbye and hello.
As we wave up.

America, I Won't Give Up on You

Because I have a type, because I read your stories,
devoured your songs since childhood, from hearing

an older cousin hum "Hello I Love You" by The Doors,
"Modern Love" by Bowie, "All of My Love" by Zeppelin,

"I Think I Love You" by the Partridge family,
which sounds like the Patriarch family,

which sounds like the Patriotic family,
which sounds like America, final inning swinging

that bat, I'm still waiting for you to shift, America,
give up your reckless ways. You keep promising

change while hanging onto old habits. Too in love
with yourself, or addicted to what corporations sold

us when we were young. Because I have a type,
I'm into the scar over your left eye, America.

Sign of a dagger on your neck you say is a birthmark?
That's sexy. The way a pool hall posing as a bookclub

shaking down fascist ideas is sexy, or a furniture store
offering midafternoon naps is sexy.

America, you once had a popular profile on social media
but then got found out on a second date.

The way you react to speeding tickets, or when a server
brings the wrong order. America makes

a strong first impression: chiseled features, witty banter,
a penchant for debate—

and who doesn't want to cruise through its towns
with photo-worthy statues studied in art history,

managed by smiles made whiter by bleach
appearing slightly better looking, to get more votes?

It's a two-party system blaring outdated music
over loudspeakers that will become landfill.

Ain't that America. But hear me out.
I used to love you, and still do love

your movies, your three-chord hits,
denim jean history and Gibson guitars.

I love your painted toenails, man buns,
and rainbow parades.

I love your vast and ever-changing terrain
driving from one side to another.

I love the car you made to drive, blasting
eighty years of rock' n' roll on the ride west.

I know there are other places far less obvious
about their dysfunctions.

I know not everyone needs to be in the spotlight
all the time like you do, America.

You are the troublemaker during holidays,
loudmouth at family gatherings,

and when the unhappiest of your cousins
gets a shotgun and mixes in a bad idea:

like nobody loves me,
like something is wrong here,

like school is the problem,
like an airplane through a tower,

that's when I want to fix you America—
like a Coldplay song.

Lately, America, you are more
American Psycho than *America the Beautiful.*

I want to see you take off that suit and meet me
at the non-denominational place of prayer and peace.

I want to see you find that surplus of money
and give it away to the poorest among us.

I want to see all your favorite colors come together
in a round of *Kumbuya* meets *thunderstruck.*

America, I am asking you to be the bad boy I can trust
as you excommunicate the language of *bro,*

any need for dominance, keeping
your muscles flexed and gender open,

cause *I've got a blank space*, baby.
Be it Beyonce or Swift,

no one can hold a candle to your torch.
Just keep it lit, if you get my drift.

Oh America,
I want it all just like you.

I want you all to myself, too, except when
we hang on weekends with my friends.

People rave about your cities and countryside,
you've got a honey-sweet B-side,

you've got strings of lights from east to west,
dance halls and jazz.

You've got Miles and miles
of yellow brick highways,

you've got baseball and bourbon,
Broadway, Bukowski,

revolution and suffrage, suffering to overcome.
I'm surely leaving something and someone out,

but that's you too, America,
with your history amnesia,

fleeting cultural touchstones like the height of
today's socks or yesterday's Haight Street rock.

America, with your golden arches and just do it slay,
restitution that's coming one day.

There's always so much more to say to you.
Just know that I won't give up on you,

America, in this madding world
we call home.

About the Author

Kathleen Florence is a Los Angeles-based poet and visual artist whose work spans screen, stage and page. Her work has appeared in *Cultural Daily, Paris Lit Up, Otoliths, Arteidolia*, and in anthologies from Three Rooms Press, Great Weather for Media, and Mystic Boxing Commission. She is the co-director of Poet Film Stage and a recipient of grants from the Ontario and Canada Arts Councils. Her films and visual art have been presented internationally including at L.A.'s Barnsdall Gallery, New York's A.I.R. Gallery, Quebec City's Folie Gallery and the Asia Culture Centre in Gwanju, South Korea. *Prayers With a Side of Cash* is her debut full-length poetry collection.

Acknowledgements

These poems first appeared in the following publications:

"The Thing About Alice" *Suitcase of Chrysanthemums*,
    Great Weather for Media
"Thick Skin Bias" *The Sparring Artists / Sparring with Beatnik
    Ghosts #2*, Mystic Boxing Commission
"If War + Peace Was a Hit on Netflix" *Maintenant 17 A Journal
    of Contemporary DADA Writing & Art*, Three Rooms Press
"Edge of the Universe" *swifts & slows*, Arteidolia
"Old Lady Yoga" *swifts & slows*, Arteidolia

Deep bows to the people who have made this journey possible,
starting with Rich Ferguson, who I would drive across galaxies for.

Moon Tide Press publisher, editor, and poet Eric Morago, poet
and former editor at *Cultural Daily* Alexis Rhone Fancher, poet
and producer of Library Girl Susan Hayden, Los Angeles poets
and editors S.A. Griffin, Richard Modiano, Daniel Yaryan, the
Sunday poetry workshop crew (Nicelle Davis, Aruni Wijesinghe,
Alexandra Umlas, Jeremy Ra, Nancy Beagle, Terri Niccum,
Elaine Mintzer, Julissa Cardenas, Patti Scruggs, P.K., Jesse James,
Mackenzie Green, Melanie Perish), Poet Film Stage participants
Lynne Thompson, Michelle Bitting, Phil Abrams, Amy Raasch,
Brendan Constantine, David A. Romero, Harry E. Northup, Bob
Holman, Matt Sedillo, Beyond Baroque's Quentin Ring, jimmy
vega, Iván Salinas, Genesis Perez and Eric Ahlberg; New York
poets and editors Randee Silv, Patrick Brennan, Kat Georges, Peter
Carlaftes, Jane Ormerod, Peter Darrell, David Lawton, George
Wallace, Nicca Ray, Yuko Otomo and the late Steve Dalanchinsky,
Fausto Grossi Terenzio, Valaparaiso Foundation in Spain for
my residency, Tiny Theatre actors Rachel Burttram Powers and
Brendan Powers who inspired "Monologue", Pamela Wallace-
LaCava, soon to be grown up EE, friends, teachers and neighbors
of my Larchmont community, Kelly Gray, Christian Georgescu,
Christine Jordan, Elena Secota, Ellyn Maybe, Annie Wood, film
and drumming star Butch Norton, Amy Bremner, Greg Beaver,

Canadian artists Jacob Wren, Melanie McCall, Ron Rooth, Ian Malone, Graham Flett, Nicole De Brabandere, Danielle Grogan, bill bissett, David Bateman, Stephanie Corrin, Pixie Cram, Kathleen McCreery, An Kosurko, Bruce Kaufman, Meg Freer, Christine Mylks, Rew MacCrimmon, Dawn Cooper, Ermina Pérez, Bill Barrs, AMZ and Bob Romeo, Amanda and Peter Rigby, Beverly Brett, Chris Thompson, Hannah Riding, Sasha Fretz, Ann MacDonald, my Reichelt, Rowswell, Rogers and Ferguson clan, especially Dave Owen, the kind hearts of Hospice Care Ottawa, the late Richard Simpson, Mrs. MacKinnon, friends that reach back to days of passing dreams to each other on folded paper, and most of all to my late mother and father. See you at 1.

Also Available from Moon Tide Press

Somewhere, a Playground, Rich Ferguson (2025)
The Tautology of Water, Giovanni Boskovich (2025)
Take Care, Mark Danowsky (2025)
Dilapitatia, Kelly Gray (2025)
Reluctant Prophets, J.D. Isip (2025)
Enormous Blue Umbrella, Donna Hilbert (2025)
Sky Leaning Toward Winter, Terri Niccum (2024)
Living the Sundown: A Caregiving Memoir, G. Murray Thomas (2024)
Figure Study, Kathryn de Lancellotti (2024)
Suffer for This: Love, Sex, Marriage, & Rock 'N' Roll, Victor D. Infante (2024)
What Blooms in the Dark, Emily J. Mundy (2024)
Fable, Bryn Wickerd (2024)
Diamond Bars 2, David A. Romero (2024)
Safe Handling, Rebecca Evans (2024)
More Jerkumstances: New & Selected Poems, Barbara Eknoian (2024)
Dissection Day, Ally McGregor (2023)
He's a Color Until He's Not, Christian Hanz Lozada (2023)
The Language of Fractions, Nicelle Davis (2023)
Paradise Anonymous, Oriana Ivy (2023)
Now You Are a Missing Person, Susan Hayden (2023)
Maze Mouth, Brian Sonia-Wallace (2023)
Tangled by Blood, Rebecca Evans (2023)
Another Way of Loving Death, Jeremy Ra (2023)
Kissing the Wound, J.D. Isip (2023)
Feed It to the River, Terhi K. Cherry (2022)
Beat Not Beat: An Anthology of California Poets Screwing on the Beat and Post-Beat Tradition (2022)
When There Are Nine: Poems Celebrating the Life and Achievements of Ruth Bader Ginsburg (2022)
The Knife Thrower's Daughter, Terri Niccum (2022)
2 Revere Place, Aruni Wijesinghe (2022)
Here Go the Knives, Kelsey Bryan-Zwick (2022)
Trumpets in the Sky, Jerry Garcia (2022)

Threnody, Donna Hilbert (2022)
A Burning Lake of Paper Suns, Ellen Webre (2021)
Instructions for an Animal Body, Kelly Gray (2021)
Head *V* Heart: New & Selected Poems, Rob Sturma (2021)
Sh!t Men Say to Me: A Poetry Anthology in Response to Toxic Masculinity (2021)
Flower Grand First, Gustavo Hernandez (2021)
Everything is Radiant Between the Hates, Rich Ferguson (2020)
When the Pain Starts: Poetry as Sequential Art, Alan Passman (2020)
This Place Could Be Haunted If I Didn't Believe in Love, Lincoln McElwee (2020)
Impossible Thirst, Kathryn de Lancellotti (2020)
Lullabies for End Times, Jennifer Bradpiece (2020)
Crabgrass World, Robin Axworthy (2020)
Contortionist Tongue, Dania Ayah Alkhouli (2020)
The only thing that makes sense is to grow, Scott Ferry (2020)
Dead Letter Box, Terri Niccum (2019)
Tea and Subtitles: Selected Poems 1999-2019, Michael Miller (2019)
At the Table of the Unknown, Alexandra Umlas (2019)
The Book of Rabbits, Vince Trimboli (2019)
Everything I Write Is a Love Song to the World, David McIntire (2019)
Letters to the Leader, HanaLena Fennel (2019)
Darwin's Garden, Lee Rossi (2019)
Dark Ink: A Poetry Anthology Inspired by Horror (2018)
Drop and Dazzle, Peggy Dobreer (2018)
Junkie Wife, Alexis Rhone Fancher (2018)
The Moon, My Lover, My Mother, & the Dog, Daniel McGinn (2018)
Lullaby of Teeth: An Anthology of Southern California Poetry (2017)
Angels in Seven, Michael Miller (2016)
A Likely Story, Robbi Nester (2014)
Embers on the Stairs, Ruth Bavetta (2014)
The Green of Sunset, John Brantingham (2013)
The Savagery of Bone, Timothy Matthew Perez (2013)
The Silence of Doorways, Sharon Venezio (2013)
Cosmos: An Anthology of Southern California Poetry (2012)
Straws and Shadows, Irena Praitis (2012)

In the Lake of Your Bones, Peggy Dobreer (2012)
I Was Building Up to Something, Susan Davis (2011)
Hopeless Cases, Michael Kramer (2011)
One World, Gail Newman (2011)
What We Ache For, Eric Morago (2010)
Now and Then, Lee Mallory (2009)
Pop Art: An Anthology of Southern California Poetry (2009)
In the Heaven of Never Before, Carine Topal (2008)
A Wild Region, Kate Buckley (2008)
Carving in Bone: An Anthology of Orange County Poetry (2007)
Kindness from a Dark God, Ben Trigg (2007)
A Thin Strand of Lights, Ricki Mandeville (2006)
Sleepyhead Assassins, Mindy Nettifee (2006)
Tide Pools: An Anthology of Orange County Poetry (2006)
Lost American Nights: Lyrics & Poems, Michael Ubaldini (2006)

Patrons

Moon Tide Press would like to thank the following people for their support in helping publish the finest poetry from the Southern California region. To sign up as a patron, visit www.moontidepress. com or send an email to publisher@moontidepress.com.

Anonymous
Robin Axworthy
Conner Brenner
Nicole Connolly
Bill Cushing
Susan Davis
Kristen Baum DeBeasi
Peggy Dobreer
Kate Gale
Dennis Gowans
Alexis Rhone Fancher
HanaLena Fennel
Half Off Books & Brad T. Cox
Donna Hilbert
Jim & Vicky Hoggatt
Michael Kramer
Ron Koertge & Bianca Richards
Gary Jacobelly
Ray & Christi Lacoste

Jeffery Lewis
Zachary & Tammy Locklin
Lincoln McElwee
David McIntire
José Enrique Medina
Michael Miller & Rachanee Srisavasdi
Michelle & Robert Miller
Ronny & Richard Morago
Terri Niccum
Andrew November
Jeremy Ra
Luke & Mia Salazar
Jennifer Smith
Roger Sponder
Andrew Turner
Rex Wilder
Mariano Zaro
Wes Bryan Zwick